People of the Bible

The Bible through stories and pictures

St. Peter
and St. Paul

Copyright © in this format Belitha Press Ltd 1985

Text copyright © Catherine Storr 1985

Illustrations copyright © Mark Peppé 1985

Art Director: Treld Bicknell

First published in Great Britain in paperback 1985
by Methuen Children's Books Ltd,
11 New Fetter Lane, London EC4P 4EE

 Conceived, designed and produced by Belitha Press Ltd,
2 Beresford Terrace, London N5 2DH

ISBN 0 416 49190 1

Printed in Hong Kong
by South China Printing Co.

St. Peter and St. Paul

Retold by Catherine Storr

Pictures by Mark Peppé

Methuen Children's Books
in association with Belitha Press Ltd

After Jesus had been put to death,
his disciples were very sad. They thought at first
that they would never see him again.
But on the third day after he had been killed,
he rose from the dead.
Mary Magdalene, who had loved him very much,
saw him in the garden of the tomb
where he had been buried.
She told the disciples that he had spoken to her.
They could not believe her,
until they had seen Jesus again for themselves.

One night, Peter and John and some other disciples
went to fish on the Sea of Galilee.
But they caught nothing. Early the next morning,
they saw someone standing on the shore,
but they did not know who it was.
The person said,
'Cast your net on the right side of the ship.'

The disciples did this,
and found they could not draw the net in,
it was so heavy with fish.
John said to the others, 'That is Jesus.'
When Peter heard this, he jumped into the sea
and swam to the shore.
The others followed in a little boat,
dragging the net after them.

Jesus had made a fire on the shore. He said,
'Come and dine.' He gave them bread and fish to eat.
Presently he said to Peter, 'Do you love me?'
Peter said, 'Yes, Lord, you know I do.'
Jesus said, 'Feed my lambs.'
Twice more Jesus asked Peter, 'Do you love me?'
Each time, Peter said, 'Yes, Lord, you know I do.'
Then Peter remembered that after Jesus was taken
by the soldiers to be tried and killed,
he had said three times that he did not know Jesus.

He remembered, too, that once
Jesus had said to him, 'Peter, you are blessed.
You are the rock
on which the Christian church will be founded.'
He meant that Peter was the follower
who Jesus believed would start the Christian Church.
The name Peter, means 'rock' or 'stone'.

After this, Peter and John and James,
went with the other disciples to many places,
teaching about Jesus.
They healed a great many people.
They and their followers shared everything they had,
food, clothes and money,
so that no one was hungry or cold.
The people used to bring their ill friends
to lie where Peter's shadow might fall on them.
They believed that this would be enough
to make them well.

One of the men who followed the disciples
and believed in their teaching,
was a Greek called Stephen.
The High Priests and elders of the temple were angry
that he also preached about Jesus,
and healed people. They paid some people to say
that Stephen had been speaking against God.
They took him outside the city and stoned him to death.

A young Jewish man, called Paul,
stood there, watching Stephen die.
He was pleased, because he hated the Christians
who followed the teachings of Jesus.
The men who were stoning Stephen
had left Paul to look after their clothes.

Paul continued to persecute the Christians.
He set out for Damascus,
meaning to bring Christians back
as prisoners to Jerusalem.
On the road to Damascus,
suddenly, a great light shone round him.
He fell to the earth, and heard a voice calling,
'Paul, why do you persecute me?'
Paul trembled and said, 'Who are you?'
The voice said, 'I am Jesus.
Get up and go into the city.'
For three days after this, Paul was blind.
Then God gave him back his sight.

Now Paul believed that Jesus was the son of God
and he went about preaching and teaching about him.
The Jews were angry when they heard of this.
They watched the gates of Damascus
by day and by night
so that they could catch him and kill him.
But the disciples let him down
over a wall, at night, in a basket.
When Paul reached Jerusalem,
he wanted to join the other Christians.
But they were afraid of him, until they heard
how he had preached boldly about Jesus in Damascus.

Soon after this, Herod, the King of Judaea,
decided to kill Peter, to please the Jews.
He threw him into prison,
guarded by four groups of soldiers.
He meant to kill him after Easter.
The night before Peter was to be killed,
as he lay asleep, a great light shone in the prison.

The angel of the Lord
struck Peter on the side and said,
'Get up quickly.
Put on your sandals and your clothes.'
The chains fell off Peter's hands,
and he followed the angel out of the prison.
As they went, the prison gates opened by themselves.

Paul travelled to many different countries,
preaching and healing the sick,
and everywhere he had been, he left new groups of
Christians.
When he was in Jerusalem, the Jews turned him out
of the temple.
The captain of the guard bound Paul's hands
and took him to the castle.
'Let me speak to you,' Paul said.
'Can you speak Greek? Aren't you an Egyptian?'
the captain asked.
Paul said, 'I am a Jew from Tarsus,
and I am a citizen of no mean city.
Are you also a Roman?'
The captain said, 'Yes,
but I had to pay a great price for it.'
Paul said, 'I was free born, a citizen of Rome'.

Paul was brought before two Governors of Judaea.
The first who questioned him was Felix,
who allowed him to live in Jerusalem,
free to see his friends.
Two years later a new Governor, Festus,
questioned Paul.
Paul said, 'I have not offended
against the laws of the Jews,
nor against the laws of Caesar.
Caesar should judge me.'
Festus sent Paul to stand before Agrippa, the King.
After Agrippa had heard Paul speak, he said,
'You almost persuade me to become a Christian.'

It was decided that Paul should be sent to Rome.

He and Luke, a doctor, and other prisoners
were guarded by soldiers,
and they embarked on a ship
which took them first to Sidon.
From there, because the winds were against them,
they sailed by Cyprus to the city of Myra.

There they found a ship from Alexandria
which would take them to Italy.
They sailed slowly for many days
and reached Crete. Now the winter was coming
and Paul warned the captain and the soldiers
that it was too dangerous to go further,
but the master of the ship was determined to go on.
After they had left Crete,
a tempest drove the ship before it
towards dangerous quicksands.
There was no sun nor stars to steer by
and everyone on board the ship
thought that they must die.

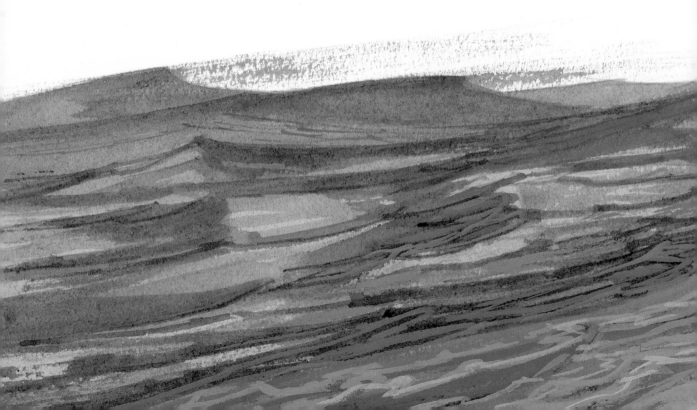

Then Paul spoke to them. 'Be of good cheer.
No man shall lose his life, but we must lose the ship,
when we are cast upon a certain island.'
At last, one night,
as the ship was driven up and down by the wind,
the sailors found that they were near land.
Some of the sailors wanted to escape
in the small boat, but Paul said,
'You can only be saved if you stay in the ship.'
As day broke, Paul told the men
to eat to give them strength.
They then threw out the cargo to lighten the ship.

They saw an unknown shore,
with a creek where they thought they might land.
They hoisted the mainsail, and ran the ship to ground.
The front of the ship stuck fast,
but the back was broken up.
Then the sailors and the soldiers and the prisoners
swam to the beach, some alone,
others with planks of wood from the ship.
They had landed on the island of Malta.
Some time later Paul at last reached Rome,
where he was allowed to live outside the prison
and to teach people about the Christian Church.

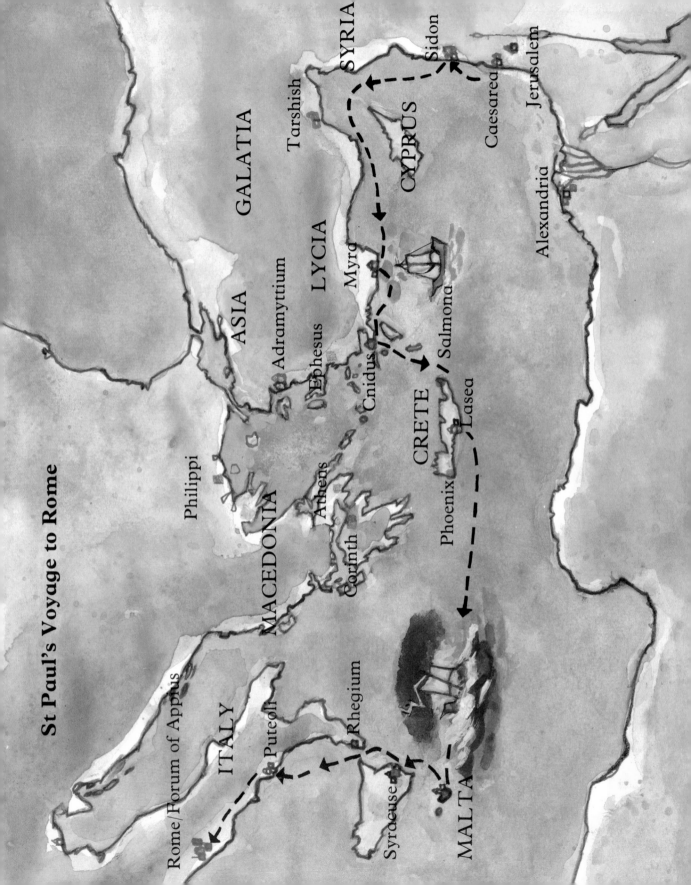

St Paul's Voyage to Rome

ITALY
Rome/Forum of Appius
Puteoli
Rhegium
Syracuse
MALTA

MACEDONIA
Philippi
Athens
Corinth

GALATIA
ASIA
Adramyttium
Ephesus
LYCIA
Myra
Cnidus
CRETE
Phoenix
Lasea
Salmona

Tarshish
SYRIA
Sidon
CYPRUS
Caesarea
Jerusalem
Alexandria